A Young Citizen's Guide To:

The Media in Politics

Julian Petley

HODDER
Wayland

an imprint of Hodder Children's Books

A Young Citizen's Guide series
Parliament
Local Government
The Electoral System
Central Government
The Criminal Justice System
Voluntary Groups
The Media in Politics
The European Union
Money
Political Parties

© Copyright 2002 Hodder Wayland

Published in Great Britain in 2002 by Hodder Wayland,
an imprint of Hodder Children's Books

Editor: Patience Coster
Series editor: Alex Woolf
Series design: Simon Borrough
Picture research: Glass Onion Pictures
Consultant: Dr Stephen Coleman

British Library Cataloguing in Publication Data
A young citizen's guide to the media in politics
1. Press and politics - Great Britain - Juvenile literature
2. Mass media - Political aspects - Great Britain -
Juvenile literature
I. Title II. The media in politics

302.2'3'0941

ISBN 0 7502 3780 5

Printed and bound in Hong
Kong by C&C

Hodder Children's Books,
a division of Hodder Headline
Limited, 338 Euston Road,
London NW1 3BH

Picture acknowledgements:
the publisher would like to thank
the following for permission to
reproduce their pictures:
Camera Press 9 (Stewart Mark);
Eye Ubiquitous 29 (Steve
Lindridge); John Frost Historical
Newspaper Service 11; Hodder
Wayland Picture Library 12, 13
(top); Impact 10 (Stefano de
Luigi/Editing), 17 (Mark Cator);
Photofusion 28 (Peter Olive);
Popperfoto 6, 13 (bottom), 14,
16, 20, 22, 24-5; Popperfoto/
Reuters 4, 5, 7 (Mel Nudelman),
18, 23, 26; Press Association 19
(Fiona Hanson), *title page* and
27; Science Photo Library 8
(David Parker); Topham
Picturepoint 15, *contents page*
and 21.

Cover: Iain Duncan Smith facing
the press (Popperfoto); Charles
Kennedy speaking in party
debate (Popperfoto); Newspaper
headlines (Popperfoto); Tony
Blair addressing the media in
Downing Street (Popperfoto).

Contents

What are the Media?

The media are the main means of communication in the modern world. They have become so numerous and so central to our daily lives that it is often said that we now live in a 'media environment'. Up until the eighteenth century, most communication in Britain took place on a face-to-face basis, especially among those who could not read or write. However, in Western societies today, a vast range of other forms of communication exists. These are frequently referred to as the mass media – 'mass' because they can communicate with huge numbers of people at once, and 'media' because they are *mediated*. This means that they are indirect forms of communication which involve various kinds of complex technology in order to put their message across.

A window on the world? If we consider how much we think we know about our society, and about the world in general, we find that most of our views are actually based not upon direct personal experience but on second-hand media accounts. If we think of all the firm opinions we have about people we've never met and are never likely to meet – from Tony Blair to Posh and Becks – we soon realize that we have the media to thank for shaping these opinions. And if we then go on to think about how these second-hand accounts – or *representations* – of our world are routinely organized and structured, we may begin to ask ourselves certain questions. For example:

Stars in the news: Victoria and David Beckham.

- Why are all the papers and news programmes covering much the same stories, even if the coverage itself often varies in tone and style?
- Why are these particular stories, and not others, judged to be 'newsworthy' by all the media?
- Are political personalities looming larger than political issues?

- Are minor domestic political stories being given more space than major foreign ones?
- Why is there nothing about where I live and the issues that matter to me?

These are some of the questions that this book, which focuses on the relationship between the UK political system and the media, will seek to answer.

In the aftermath of the attack on the World Trade Centre in New York on 11 September 2001, newspapers were an important source of information and opinion about the bombing and its consequences.

The popular press

The first mass medium was print journalism, or the popular press. Newspapers and magazines became widely available in the eighteenth century, as an increasing number of people not only learned to read but also had money to spend on goods and services. This made them attractive to those who provided the goods and services, who advertised them in the press. This financial support from advertising greatly aided the media's development.

The birth of television

In 1922 the BBC (British Broadcasting Company, which became the British Broadcasting Corporation in 1927) began transmitting regular radio broadcasts, with television transmissions following in the 1930s. But these television broadcasts reached only a limited audience, as TV sets were extremely expensive and the transmissions were not powerful enough to be received across the entire country. It was not until the mid-1950s, when the general public had more money to spend and when, in 1955, Independent Television (ITV) arrived, that television in Britain began to become a truly mass medium. The television channel BBC2 followed in 1964, and Channel 4 in 1982. In 1990, the Broadcasting Act encouraged new broadcasters to enter the field, and the decade saw the arrival of a number of satellite and cable television services, as well as Channel 5 in 1997. This

Early television sets were expensive and prized possessions, and the screens were considerably smaller than those of today's models.

opening up of broadcasting was known as 'deregulation'. Home video came into being in 1979, but by 2000 the videocassette began to face the challenge of the DVD.

Convergence The most far-reaching addition to our media environment in the late twentieth century was undoubtedly the home computer. To begin with, in the early 1980s, most domestic computers were little more than elaborate typewriters and calculators. It was not until the late 1980s and the start of the 1990s that they really entered the media scene. At this point, the process of 'convergence' began, in other words, the coming together of the once separate broadcasting and telecommunications services – the union of the television, telephone and home computer. Convergence means that the telephone, once merely a voice-carrying device, can, when hooked up to a computer, carry any kind of information, from words and graphics to music and movies. No longer are the various forms of communications technology fenced off from one another in separate compartments. These technologies are now all connected and capable of carrying and transmitting the same kind of information.

Convergence was made possible by several factors. The market for conventional media products, such as televisions and radios, had become saturated. In other words, most people already owned the media goods they felt they needed, and did not wish to replace them. This posed a problem for the world's vast electronic industries, which turned to conquering new non-Western markets, such as South America and the Indian sub-continent, and developing new products, and in particular domestic computers, in the West.

The year 2000 saw the merger of one of the world's leading internet service providers – AOL – with one of its largest media groups – Time Warner.

7

Fibre optics Up until this point, even the simplest computer was both too large and too expensive for the average home, but the mass production of microchips made vast, hitherto undreamed-of computer power available to the ordinary consumer. At the same time, new kinds of cabling known as fibre optics were being developed, which made it possible for huge amounts of information to be communicated at staggering speeds *between* computers.

In addition to these technological developments were important political ones. Up until the 1980s, in Britain and the rest of Europe, national governments generally agreed that the provision of broadcasting and telecommunications was a 'natural monopoly'. In other words, it was something best left to single organizations, or a very few carefully regulated ones. It was also felt that these things were so important to society that they should not be left entirely to private business whose main priority was to make a profit rather than perform a public service. Since broadcasting and telecommunications were regarded as 'public services', they were run as public corporations in the public interest. Most of the broadcast media therefore escaped being placed in the hands of private companies whose first loyalty was to their shareholders, not to the public.

Lobbying However, during the 1980s, large media companies such as Rupert Murdoch's News Corporation urged individual European governments and the European Commission to be allowed into the broadcasting and telecommunications sectors, which they saw as being potentially extremely profitable. This highly

Fibre optic cables enable vast amounts of information to be transmitted instantly along wires as thin as a human hair.

'Monopoly is a terrible thing, until you have it.'
Rupert Murdoch.

organized campaign of pressure and persuasion, an
excellent example of what is known as 'lobbying',
met with a good deal of success across the
continent, particularly in Britain. Here, it was
extremely well matched by the kind of deregulatory,
more commercially-minded policies that were
pursued by Conservative governments in the 1980s
and 1990s. Since the Conservatives' fall from
power in 1997, the Labour government has
pursued similar policies in the fields of broadcasting
and telecommunications.

Newspaper tycoon
Rupert Murdoch became
a powerful new figure in
UK broadcasting during
the 1990s.

The important lesson of this particular story is that the media do not simply reflect the political debates that take place in society, both in Parliament and outside it – they are themselves a crucial part of it. While it is certainly true that the media today provide politicians with one of their most important means of putting across their ideas to the population at large, it is also the case that the media need a supportive political environment in which to flourish.

Government involvement in the media

The government sets the level of the BBC licence fee, which all television viewers are supposed to pay, and on which the BBC depends largely for its income. If the level is too low, the BBC finds it that much more difficult to make programmes and has to cut back on staff and resources. In the case of ITV and Channel 4, the government sets the level of taxation on the profits they receive from carrying advertising. This is known as the 'levy'. If the levy is set too high, there is that much less money available to make television programmes. The government also requires the broadcasters to establish, and obey, various codes of practice which govern what is and is not permissible in the programmes they make or buy. At the same time, the broadcasters, like the other media, have to obey the laws governing libel, official secrecy, obscenity, and so on. Meanwhile, the press has long been concerned to prove to government that its own system of internal 'self-regulation', which is run by the Press Complaints Commission, is working properly so that government does not impose any system of external or independent regulation upon it.

Silvio Berlusconi, media magnate and now Italian prime minister. Not altogether surprisingly, certain media owners want to see restrictions on media ownership reduced so that they can develop their media empires still further.

How the Media Entered Politics

As the media developed, their potential political importance became increasingly clear to politicians, as well as to those who worked in the media. Politicians often tried to limit what they saw as the media's political powers, but were also keen to use them for their own ends when it suited them. Meanwhile, many people working in the media tried to withstand what they saw as political interference and to extend the bounds of media freedom.

Censorship and taxes In Britain, as in most European countries, the early press was subjected to strict political and religious censorship. By the beginning of the eighteenth century, however, the *direct* power of the state and the church over the press had begun to weaken, not least because of the sheer amount of printed material then being produced. Nonetheless, that century also saw the government introduce taxes on advertising revenue, which was a very important source of income for newspapers.

The government also brought in a tax known as a 'stamp duty' on every copy of a newspaper sold. These taxes were clearly intended to keep newspaper cover prices relatively high. In this way, press readership would be restricted to the better off members of society, and a degree of government control over the industry would be preserved. At this time there was a widespread fear in political circles that the growth of socialist, working-class newspapers such as *The Poor Man's Guardian, The Liberator, Black Dwarf* and *Twopenny Trash* would only add to the political unrest that was growing among the working class.

The front cover of *The Poor Man's Guardian*, an early radical newspaper.

A new phase In the mid-nineteenth century these increasingly unpopular 'taxes on knowledge', as they came to be known, were abolished. On the one hand, this was because they were increasingly resisted. On the other, the government began to realize that if rich and powerful industrialists could control the production of cheap, mass-circulation newspapers, they might defeat the socialist press far more effectively than taxes had ever done – in the marketplace. They would do this either by tempting away their readers, or by raising the costs of producing a newspaper, or a combination of the two.

The successful entrance of the 'men of capital and respectability' into the newspaper market resulted in distinct changes in the way in which newspapers were produced. The introduction of the new technology needed to print mass-circulation newspapers meant that production and operating costs soared. But while this made newspapers more expensive to produce, mass-market newspapers could be sold extremely cheaply because they were subsidized by advertising. Meanwhile, many socialist papers were either priced out of the market, forced to close, moderate their socialism, or confine themselves to readership by a minority of people.

Newspapers were sold in a variety of ways in the early twentieth century.

Guarding the public interest

The nineteenth century saw the birth of newspapers as we know them today. These were run for profit by large private companies, which usually had many other interests both inside and outside the media. They were generally critical of movements, people or ideas that challenged the established order, and

'[Repeal would] **create a cheap press in the hands of men of good moral character, of respectability, and of capital ... [and would give them] the power of gaining access by newspapers, by faithful record of the facts, to the minds of the working classes.'**
In 1854 Thomas Milner-Gibson, the president of the Association for the Repeal of the Taxes on Knowledge, argued in favour of the repeal of taxes on newspapers.

divided into the 'serious' and 'popular' papers (now described as 'broadsheet' and 'tabloid'). This era also established the press in a curiously contradictory position. Although the press was a powerful political and economic interest in its own right, it was also – at least in the eyes of many of the journalists working in it – a watchdog over those in positions of power and influence and a guardian of the public interest. It was in this latter role, for example, that a newspaper such as the *Guardian* in the 1990s exposed the fact that certain MPs were being paid by private companies to ask parliamentary questions that furthered those companies' business interests.

The larger we open the field of general instruction, the firmer the foundations on which the order, the loyalty and good conduct of the lower classes will rest'.
The Home Secretary, Lord Palmerston, speaking in 1854.

Lord Beaverbrook, a press magnate who didn't hesitate to use his newspapers to spread his own political views when it suited him.

The home of the British press, Fleet Street, London, during the 1930s. In the latter part of the twentieth century, many newspaper offices moved further east, to Docklands.

Public service broadcasting

Newspapers in Britain have traditionally been regarded as their owners' private property and, within the limits of the law, theirs to do with as they like. However the airwaves in Britain have generally been seen as public property, and broadcasting itself as a public service to be run in the interests of the general public.

This has meant that broadcasting in Britain has always been either publicly owned, like the BBC, or, if privately owned like ITV or commercial radio, regulated by organizations such as the Independent Television Commission (ITC) and the Radio Authority. Such organizations are publicly accountable, which means that programmes are required by law to remain strictly neutral and may not, except in certain rare circumstances, express their makers' political points of view. Participants in programmes can obviously express their political views, but the broadcasters have to ensure that a proper balance is struck between the competing viewpoints expressed.

However, broadcasting has long been criticized for ignoring or even treating with hostility political views that are non-mainstream or radical. This criticism has been forcefully expressed over the years by,

A busy control room in the early days of ITV.

among many others, people who have gone on strike in order to preserve their jobs or improve their working conditions, those campaigning for a re-united Ireland, black people, sexual minorities, and, more recently, anti-globalization campaigners.

The General Strike

In 1926 there was a General Strike in Britain, and many people feared that the Russian Revolution of 1917 was about to repeat itself here. The outbreak of the strike coincided with the earliest days of the BBC, led by its formidable head John (later Lord) Reith. There were those in government who wanted to take over the BBC (as they would have been entitled to do) and run it as a straightforward vehicle for spreading views opposed to the strike. However, the government decided that an apparently independent BBC might better serve the anti-strike cause. Behind the scenes, the government simply prevented Reith from allowing the Archbishop of Canterbury and the leader of the Labour Party to broadcast on the BBC views which might have been even mildly critical of the government and sympathetic to the strikers.

A police officer tries to keep transport running during the General Strike of 1926.

A national institution Reith justified the BBC's behaviour by arguing that: 'assuming the BBC is for the people, and that the government is for the people, then the BBC must be for the government in this crisis'. But what of the large numbers of 'the people' who were on strike? The answer to this question, for Reith, lay in the fact that the strike had been declared illegal. As a national institution, the BBC, he argued: 'had to assist in the maintaining of the essential services of the country, the preservation of law and order, and the life and liberty of the individual and the community'. The requirement for 'impartiality' was applied only to political views and activities that fell within the bounds of what Parliament had deemed legitimate and legal. As far as the BBC was concerned, the strikers were acting outside those boundaries.

This may all seem a long time ago now, but most broadcasting historians would agree that the ground rules for broadcasting in the UK were laid with the BBC's coverage of the General Strike.

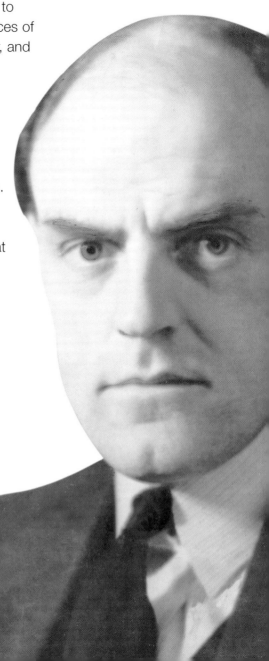

Lord Reith, the first and most famous Director General of the BBC.

'The arrangements made by the BBC to cover the event [the General Strike] defined the nature of its "independence" and laid down the framework within which broadcasters and ministers have negotiated ever since – a framework described as allowing the corporation liberty on parole.'
Kevin Williams in his book *Get Me a Murder a Day!*, explaining that broadcasters are free to do as they like – as long as they don't step seriously out of line!

How Politicians Try to Influence the Media

In our society, the media play a key role in communicating the political developments of the day. It is hardly surprising, therefore, that politicians, whether in government or opposition, try to appear in the media as often as possible. They also work to ensure that their policies achieve maximum media exposure and are portrayed in the best possible light.

Downing Street in London is a favourite haunt of press photographers.

Like other organizations keen to put their messages across to the media, political parties constantly produce for journalists easily digested snippets of news (known as press releases) and frequently hold press conferences. Politicians need to talk to the media, and, in order to keep the news up to date – a steady flow of the latest news being an important selling point for the modern media – the media need to talk to politicians. This relationship between politicians and the media, in particular the terms on which politicians grant access to the media, and vice versa, has become an increasingly important aspect of the daily political process in Britain.

17

The Lobby system

One of the most important weapons that political parties (especially the party that is in power) possess in their efforts to gain favourable, and discourage unfavourable, media coverage is the Lobby system. The Lobby began in 1884 as a way of enabling newspapers' parliamentary reporters (or correspondents) to gain access to authoritative information about governmental business. The system is so named because correspondents originally assembled in the Lobby of the House of Commons. Currently there are around two hundred Lobby correspondents, and they are the major source of published and broadcast political news.

For the Lobby journalist, the most important source of political news is the Prime Minister's press secretary. He or she is a civil servant paid for by public funds and therefore, officially, not working on behalf of whichever party is in power. However, during the Conservative governments of the 1980s, the role appeared to become an increasingly party-political one, and has continued to be so under the Labour government.

Prime Minister Tony Blair personally briefs a select group of journalists.

'Briefings [are] rigged for the benefit and convenience of the givers and receivers of information and against the interests of the consumer – the reader, the listener, the viewer and the voter.'

Peter Hennessy, a leading commentator on British politics, talking about the private meetings between government press secretary and lobby correspondents.

A culture of secrecy

More than anything else it is the secretiveness of the Lobby that has increasingly brought it into disrepute. It is a system in which journalists cannot reveal the sources of their information, for fear of being banished from the Lobby. This makes it all too easy for politicians to exploit journalists for news-management purposes, known as 'spin doctoring' or media manipulation. It tends to make journalists lazy and passive, turning them into what is known as 'Lobby fodder'. In short, it could be argued that the Lobby is part of the 'culture of secrecy' which many people believe makes British politics less open and accountable than they should be.

However, these 'unattributable briefings' of Lobby journalists by the Prime Minister's press secretary, and others, may sometimes enable journalists to publish information to which no minister or official would be prepared publicly to put their name. In this sense these briefings could be seen as encouraging a degree of unofficial openness in government business. Such briefings are frequently the source of the so-called 'leaks' which so upset governments but which many people see as shedding much-needed light on the unnecessarily secretive workings of government.

Labour researcher Jo Moore was accused of spin-doctoring after suggesting to colleagues that 11 September 2001 would be a good day to announce stories that were bad news for the government. Such stories would, she said, be 'buried' by coverage of the terrorist attacks.

'[This] access to the troughs and watering holes frequented by our elected legislators places them in a unique position from which to observe and report upon the very heart of the British political system.'
Veteran journalist Ian Aitken, describing the privileged position of the Lobby correspondent.

Support system

It is equally the case that the Lobby system discourages independent journalistic initiatives. If a journalist breaks the rules of the Lobby, and is then thrown out of it, he or she is immediately cut off from the valuable information it undoubtedly supplies, and his or her job is then at risk. The way in which journalists themselves keep the Lobby system going was illustrated in 1986 when the *Guardian, Independent* and *Scotsman* voluntarily left the Lobby system in protest at the way in which the then press secretary, Bernard Ingham, was manipulating it for party-political ends. This crisis resulted in Lobby members voting on whether to keep the system of 'unattributable briefings' – and deciding to do so by a majority of 67 votes to 55. The newspapers that had left the system soon returned to it.

'Press officers speak as frankly as they feel able to members [of the Lobby], either individually or collectively, on a background basis: i.e. the journalist does not identify his source precisely in writing his story...'
The words of Bernard Ingham, government press secretary (1979-90). Some people believed that Ingham did not act as an impartial civil servant but directed political communications in the interest of the government and not of the public as a whole.

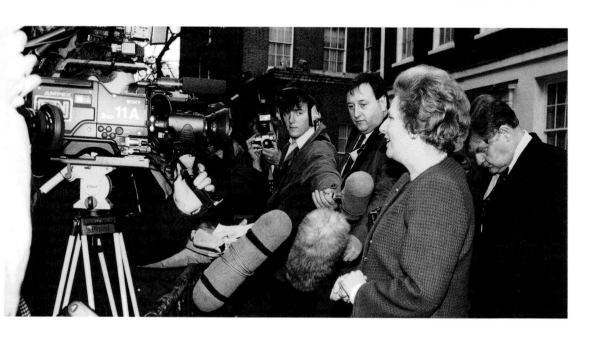

Then Prime Minister Margaret Thatcher addresses the media in 1989. Her press secretary Bernard Ingham (far right, head bowed) stands behind her.

In 2001, Iain Duncan Smith meets the media in his new role as leader of the Conservative Party.

'Lobby information is to real information roughly what sliced bread is to real food. It is cheap, conveniently packaged, with most of the goodness and wholesome character taken out of it. It is not wholly without nutritional value, but it is not as good as the real thing. But the real thing tends to be more expensive and more demanding on the palate.'
Political journalist Peter Kellner.

Perhaps unsurprisingly then, principled stands by newspapers against the Lobby system are extremely rare. It is more likely that their journalists will simply be sucked into the system, leading to the charge by leading political journalist Peter Kellner that the Lobby 'produces lazy journalism undertaken by lazy journalists'. In this respect, then, the Lobby could be seen as one of the chief means by which political news, and especially potentially unpopular or problematic news, is increasingly 'packaged' in ways that will make it palatable to the general public. And the journalists play a key role in neatly and prettily wrapping it up.

The spin doctor Since the Labour Party
came to power in 1997, the argument that the
Lobby system threatens to turn journalists from
active and critical observers of political affairs into
passive vehicles for government messages has
increasingly moved to the centre of political debate.
Prior to the 1997 election, the Labour Party had
been bruised by decades of hostile reporting in the
press, and damaged by the way in which its own
MPs had frequently 'leaked' to the media against
each other or against party policy. Doubtless
impressed also by Bernard Ingham's considerable
achievements on behalf of the Conservatives,
Labour in opposition had built itself a truly
formidable media-handling machine. This was
headed by the former tabloid journalist Alastair
Campbell, and had swung into effective operation
well before 1997.

New Labour's chief spin
doctor, Alastair Campbell (left),
chats with the formidable and
long-standing MP for
Bolsover, Dennis Skinner, at
the Labour Party conference
in 1999.

Labour's media-handling machine brought with it the notion of the 'spin doctor', although the term, which was imported from the United States, could equally well have been applied to Ingham. The role of the spin doctor received even more media attention when, after the 1997 election, Campbell became Prime Minister Tony Blair's press secretary. He then took a line with the media, as well as with Labour MPs and ministers, which many journalists regarded as bullying and, above all, too party-political.

Hypocritical? On the one

hand it might be argued that such complaints were decidedly hypocritical coming from journalists, many of whose papers had spent years

Prime Minister Tony Blair takes the opportunity to reach a Middle Eastern audience during the war in Afghanistan in 2001. Here he is interviewed by a journalist from the Qatari-based Al Jazeera television station.

'spinning' anti-Labour stories day after day in their pages. On the other, it might be said that the Conservatives had already thoroughly politicized the office of press secretary and that the Labour government was simply filling it with an appropriately political appointee.

However, it was certainly the case that Labour, in opposition, had been extremely critical of the way in which the governmental information system had become so centralized and politicized. Labour had also promised to make the British political system more open and accountable. Such a promise appeared to many to sound the death knell for secretive institutions such as the Lobby. In the event, however, little has changed, a state of affairs for which it could be argued that journalists as well as politicians are equally to blame.

How the Media Deal with Politics

There is a big difference between the ways in which the press and broadcasters cover political matters. Newspapers can and do follow a particular political 'line', while radio and television programmes are required by law to remain politically neutral. A newspaper's owner will normally set its political line. Newspaper owners appoint like-minded editors and senior managerial staff, and the journalists who work for them understand the political limits within which they are expected to work – even if they do not necessarily agree with them.

The British press marks the Labour Party's election victory in 1997.

Changing opinions Throughout the twentieth century, most British newspapers supported the Conservative Party. For example, at the 1987 general election the only daily papers to support the Labour Party were the *Mirror* and *Guardian*; the *Independent* remained uncommitted and *Today* supported the idea of a coalition consisting of the three main parties. However, ten years later, things had changed considerably. At the 1997 general election, only the *Express*, *Mail* and *Telegraph* backed the Conservatives, *The Times* urged its readers to vote for 'Euro-sceptic' candidates of whatever party, and the rest backed Labour. This meant that there were 7.9 million Labour-supporting papers in circulation, compared with 4.5 million Conservative ones. In other words, the political complexion of the British press had changed – but it was still politically unbalanced, only now the other way!

This raised yet other important questions about the role of the media in British politics. Firstly, had the previous long-standing hostility of much of the press towards Labour encouraged the party to alter its policies so that they were now politically acceptable, and economically beneficial, to those newspapers? Secondly, were traditionally Conservative papers simply lending their support temporarily to Labour for the period in which their chosen party was incapable of forming an effective government? Thirdly, had the Labour 'spin' machine simply bullied journalists into submission? Finally, have we now reached a position in which the press simply backs likely political winners? If the answer to any of these questions should turn out to be 'yes', it would cast considerable doubt on the effectiveness of the press as a supposed watchdog both on government and on other powerful institutions within our society.

The Murdoch press

The defection of Rupert Murdoch's *Sun* newspaper, long the main tabloid cheer-leader for the Conservatives under Prime Minister Margaret Thatcher (1979-1990), to the Labour cause was a significant development in the relationship between the media and politics. Certainly the *Sun* itself has never been in doubt about the political power it wields, proudly proclaiming in the wake of the Conservative victory in the 1992 general election that 'It Was the Sun Wot Won It'. But the newspaper was considerably less revealing about the reasons for its shift of political allegiance. Some suggested that Labour had assured Murdoch that, if it came to power, it would not introduce legislation that could limit the expansion of his multimedia empire. Others suggested that Labour had shifted many of its policies in directions of which Murdoch approved. Another suggestion was that the *Sun*, as a highly commercial operation, did not want to risk losing readers by backing what, by 1997, had become an extremely unpopular Conservative Party.

Media bias Despite the legal requirements for them to be impartial and balanced in their political coverage, radio and television broadcasters have frequently been criticized for not being so. They have been accused of bias – about Northern Ireland or civil unrest in British cities such as Bradford in 2001, for example – or for down-playing or even ignoring altogether certain kinds of story – for example, sizeable domestic protests over Britain's role in the Falklands, Iraq, Balkans and Afghanistan wars. However, it could be argued that this apparent bias is more unconscious than deliberate, the result of broadcasters working with a rather narrow, Westminster-based range of political views, which tends to exclude or marginalize voices not belonging to the main political parties.

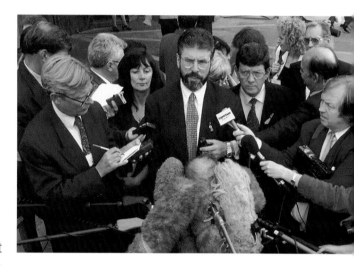

Sinn Fein leader Gerry Adams talks to the media.

However, broadcasters work in the knowledge that the government can order them not to show certain programmes or kinds of programme. Successive Broadcasting Acts have enabled the Home Secretary of the day to order the Independent Television Commission to 'refrain from broadcasting any matter or classes of matter' on commercial television. A similar clause in the BBC Licence Agreement gives the Home Secretary the same power over the BBC. This power is rarely used, but it was from 1988 until 1994 with the intention of preventing members of certain political organizations in Northern Ireland from appearing on radio and television. The government argued that this was to prevent these media giving 'extremists' the 'oxygen of publicity'.

Since 1989 parliamentary affairs in the House of Commons have been televised. This means that politicians not only have to withstand the scrutiny of their opposition colleagues, but of the general public as well.

Lightweight and trivial

Recently, the major criticism of the role played by the broadcast media in British politics has been that they have not treated politics with the seriousness and depth it deserves, and that their coverage of the political process in Britain has become increasingly lightweight and trivial. These accusations are summed up in the words 'dumbing down' and 'tabloidization' (criticisms which have also been levelled at the broadsheet press). Following the changes introduced by the 1990 Broadcasting Act, broadcasting has become more commercially competitive. This means that serious current affairs programmes, and even news bulletins, have been pushed by entertainment programmes out of primetime, early evening slots and banished late into the night. Some have been abolished altogether, or become trivial and entertainment-led 'infotainment' programmes. The question we need to ask ourselves is: do supposedly more 'viewer-friendly' news and current affairs programmes make political and other serious issues more easily understood by a wider audience, or do they simply oversimplify them and patronize the viewers?

Moving news

In 1990, the Broadcasting Act dropped ITV's obligation to show current affairs programmes in primetime slots. Famous current affairs series such as *World in Action* and *This Week* eventually vanished from the schedules. Some time later, and amid considerable political controversy, *News at Ten* was shifted from 10pm to 11pm, mainly to enable ITV to show feature films at 9pm. Not altogether surprisingly, the BBC then moved its 9pm news to 10pm, where it sometimes finds itself competing head to head with *News at Ten*, which appears to have become something of a movable feast! Meanwhile the BBC's main current affairs programme *Panorama*, once shown at 8pm on a Monday has now shifted to a Sunday late-night slot.

Do the Media Influence the ⊠ Political Process?

Judging by the extent to which politicians try not only to appear in the media but also to 'manage' the ways in which they appear there, the answer would seem to be a definite 'yes'. In recent years, politicians have seemed to care less about meeting the voters face to face, and more about creating stage-managed, camera-friendly 'media events' to appeal to voters sitting at home in front of their television sets.

In the media's defence, however, we have them to thank for the vast amount of material that is available daily, at very little cost, which can help us to become very well informed about political matters both at home and abroad. Despite the pressures to which journalists are subjected, the media are by no means always as compliant as governments would seem to wish them to be. This much was evident in the critical line taken by sections of the media in 2001 over the British government's handling of the foot and mouth crisis, and the war in Afghanistan.

Student radio stations are an excellent way for you to draw attention to and discuss political issues that are relevant to your daily life.

Influencing voters So how much influence do the media really have over people's voting patterns? While it is not the case that people vote for a particular party simply because their newspaper tells them to do so, the press may well play an important, longer-term role, along with the broadcast media, in helping to set the political agenda. However, it appears that in recent years an increasing number of people, especially young ones, have come to distrust and ignore the press and broadcasters. They have turned to 'alternative' media such as the internet, which offer news and views that have not been aired by the mainstream media. The internet also provides the opportunity for people to participate in the making and dissemination of media messages of their own. It offers all sorts of possibilities for political debate and involvement. Political parties and their representatives have their own web sites, and in some countries people can use the internet to vote on local issues in forms of 'direct democracy', known as 'electronic referenda'.

However, only a small proportion of the world's population has internet access, and many people probably prefer to use it for shopping, chatting and playing games rather than becoming politically informed and involved. And dreams about the possible political uses of the internet should not be used as an excuse for the mainstream media to slip even further away than some feel they already have from dealing with politics with the seriousness it demands. The first requirement of a democratic society is politically well-informed citizens, and the media have a crucial role to play in the provision of the information people desperately need – not just at election times, but every day of their lives.

Studying the media in school may be the first step towards a career in journalism.

Activity
Choose a major political news story and examine how it is covered by the different media. Firstly, compare how the press, radio and television deal with the story. How does television use images to tell the story? How does radio manage without them? Do newspapers run editorials, or other 'comment' pieces, along with the news story itself? Does one medium give more attention to the story than do others, and, if so, why? Secondly, compare the differences within the various media. How does the BBC's treatment of the story compare with that of the other channels? What prominence is given to the story by different papers? Is the story illustrated with pictures, and what do they add to the text? Does the paper offer its own opinion on the story? Do the tabloids and broadsheets deal with the story differently, and, if so, how?

Glossary

anti-globalization campaigner a person who is involved in protesting at the massive and ever-growing inequalities between the rich and poor countries of the world

biased one-sided or slanted

coalition a temporary alliance of different parties forming a government; the term can also be used to describe a temporary alliance of different countries

conservative opposing change

democratic a system of government which consists of representatives who are freely elected by the adult population as a whole

deregulation the abolition or weakening of rules and regulations

direct democracy another way of describing a referendum (see below)

disseminate/dissemination to distribute or spread about

DVD (Digital Video Disc or Digital Versatile Disc) a CD with images, text and music on it, a DVD is considerably more versatile, space-saving and user-friendly than a video. It also allows for better quality sound and vision, and the addition of all sorts of extra programme material.

European Commission the European Union organization that initiates policy and legislation

Euro-sceptic a person who opposes closer links with other members of the European Union (an alliance between a number of – currently fifteen – European countries)

Home Secretary the government minister in charge of the Home Office

impartiality remaining neutral or unbiased

infotainment information presented in an entertaining, and usually trivializing, fashion

libel a published statement damaging to a person's reputation

microchip a tiny flake made of silicon which holds millions of microscopic electronic components

monopoly the ownership or control by a single organization of specific goods or services

obscenity something, for example a book or a video, which a court has decided could deprave or corrupt those viewing it

official secrets those matters which a state feels it necessary to keep secret in the interests of national security

press conference a meeting organized by a business or a government department to unveil their latest initiatives to the assembled media

primetime early or mid-evening slots in the television or radio schedules, when it is assumed that audience figures will be highest

referendum (plural: referenda) the posing of a political question directly to the electorate, who then vote on it. In some countries it is possible to vote in referenda on the internet.

repeal abolish, get rid of

shareholder a person who has invested money in a company and, in turn, expects a regular share of its profits

socialist someone who believes in equality, the regulation of the market by the state, and the public ownership of certain enterprises

subsidize to support – through the payment of money by the state or a body such as the EU – producers of goods or providers of services in order to keep them in business and/or reduce the cost of those goods or services to the consumer

telecommunications the provision of telephone services

transmission the sending of the signals of which all forms of broadcasting are made up

trivial unimportant, petty or frivolous

Resources

Information books

James Curran and Jean Seaton, *Power Without Responsibility,* Routledge, 1997

Bob Franklin, *Packaging Politics,* Edward Arnold, 1994

Nicholas Jones, *Soundbites and Spin Doctors*, Cassell, 1995

Nicholas Jones, *Sultans of Spin,* Victor Gollancz, 1999

Brian McNair, *An Introduction to Political Communication*, Routledge 1999

Ralph Negrine, *Politics of the Mass Media in Britain*, Routledge, 1994

Julian Petley, *Media: The Impact On Our Lives,* Hodder Wayland, 2000

Colin Seymour-Ure, *The British Press and Broadcasting Since 1945*, Blackwell, 1996

Kevin Williams, *Get Me a Murder a Day!*, Edward Arnold, 1998

Various authors, *Mediawise series*, Hodder Wayland, 2002

The internet

http://www.dailymail.com
Web site of the *Daily Mail* newspaper (tabloid)

http://www.expressnewspapers.com
Web site of the *Daily* and *Sunday Express* newspapers (tabloids)

http://www.mirror.co.uk
Web site of the *Daily* and *Sunday Mirror* newspapers (tabloids)

http://www.thesun.co.uk
Web site of the *Sun* newspaper (tabloid)

http://www.telegraph.co.uk
Web site of the *Daily Telegraph* newspaper (broadsheet)

http:// www.ft.com
Web site of the *Financial Times* newspaper (broadsheet)

http://www.guardian.co.uk
Web site of the *Guardian* newspaper (broadsheet)

http:// www.independent.co.uk
Web site of the *Independent* newspaper (broadsheet)

http://www.the-times.co.uk
Web site of *The Times* newspaper (broadsheet)

http://www.sky.co.uk
Web site of BSkyB satellite broadcaster

http://www.bbc.co.uk
Web site of the BBC

http://www.channel4.com
Web site of Channel 4 Television

http://www.channel5.co.uk
Web site of Channel 5 Television

http://www.itc.org.uk
Web site of the Independent Television Commission

http://www.itv.co.uk
Web site of the ITV Network Centre

Index

Numbers in **bold** refer to illustrations.